IMAGES
of America

NACOGDOCHES IN WORLD WAR II

More than 100 men from Nacogdoches County died in World War II. Some were brought back home but many remain buried in cemeteries overseas, each grave marked by a simple white cross. The young deceased soldiers who came home were met at the train depot, where heads were bared, and "Taps" accompanied the rolling caisson as it traveled down Main Street on the way to the funeral home. Regardless of where they now lie, we will never forget all the brave young men and women from past and present wars who have given their lives as the ultimate sacrifice for their country. (Courtesy of Jan Dobbs Barton.)

On the Cover: Fellow soldiers accompany the body of Capt. Hiram Joseph Clark of the U.S. Army to the train depot on May 25, 1943, as he is shipped to his home in Medford, Ohio. Clark was an instructor and officer with the Women's Army Corps Branch No. 1 at Stephen F. Austin Teacher's College (SFASTC). (Courtesy of the East Texas Research Center [ETRC], Stephen F. Austin State University [SFASU].)

IMAGES
of America

NACOGDOCHES IN WORLD WAR II

Jan Dobbs Barton and Peggy Arriola Jasso

ARCADIA
PUBLISHING

ISBN 978-0-7385-7973-3

Published by Arcadia Publishing
Charleston, South Carolina

Printed in the United States of America

Library of Congress Control Number: 2010940818

For all general information, please contact Arcadia Publishing:
Telephone 843-853-2070
Fax 843-853-0044
E-mail sales@arcadiapublishing.com
For customer service and orders:
Toll-Free 1-888-313-2665

Visit us on the Internet at www.arcadiapublishing.com

This book is dedicated to the "greatest generation" of men from Nacogdoches County who suffered through the Great Depression only to leave their homes a few years later to fight in the deadliest conflict of modern history, World War II. More than 30 of these men, pictured here with the authors of this book and U.S. congressman Louie Gohmert, came together on August 14, 2010, to "Keep the Spirit of '45 Alive." We salute you! (Courtesy of Cason Monk-Metcalf Funeral Directors.)

Contents

ACKNOWLEDGMENTS

The authors gratefully acknowledge the many people who helped gather photographs and stories for this pictorial history of Nacogdoches during World War II. It has been a humbling experience to delve into this historic period of time and to hear the stories of its unsung heroes. So many people need credit, but special thanks goes to Linda Reynolds and her staff at the East Texas Research Center (ETRC), Ralph W. Steen Library at Stephen F. Austin State University. The ETRC collects, preserves, and provides physical and virtual access to East Texas's unique cultural history, and is a great resource to our community. With its assistance, we have spent countless hours reading old newspapers, accessing online collections, and browsing and scanning photographs.

Other sources of information and great joy are the local personalities who lived through the war times and have so graciously shared their experiences with us. Joyce Bright Swearingen, Francis Edward Abernethy, James "Buck" Lee, George Self, Edward Smith, James Arriola, Clarence "Bo" McMichael, and many others have been our historians. Each one holds a special place in the completion of this book.

Other sources of information are the Veterans of Foreign Wars Post No. 3873, the American Legion Post No. 3893, Robert "Bob" Sitton with the Stephen F. Austin Alumni Association, the Nacogdoches High School Alumni Association, and all the military men, their families, and their friends who have so graciously shared photographs and stories. We regret that we could not include every story and picture that was shared. Each was special and the determination of what to include was extremely difficult.

We would be remiss if we did not give special recognition to our fathers, Theodore "T. C." Dobbs Jr. and George Arriola Jr., whose service and sacrifices in World War II fueled our interest in this period. We sincerely hope that this book will honor them, as well as the many other men and women from Nacogdoches County who helped preserve our freedoms.

INTRODUCTION

From the bombing of Pearl Harbor on December 7, 1941, through the final surrender by the Japanese in Tokyo Bay on September 2, 1945, America was affected by World War II like no other event in history. During this time, more than 16 million men and women entered the U.S. military. Most fought the war in strange lands and unknown tropical islands like the Philippines, Guam, and Okinawa, and sometimes in more familiar places, like England, France, Germany, and Italy. The estimate of Americans who died during this time period is more than 400,000, with nearly 700,000 wounded and more than 130,000 taken as prisoners of war (POWs). Worldwide, the numbers vary greatly and are staggering; the estimates are between 50 and 70 million military and civilian lives lost. For this reason, World War II has been called the deadliest military conflict in history.

Nacogdoches County, like most of the nation, was suffering tough economic times when Pearl Harbor was attacked on December 7, 1941. The Great Depression of the 1930s caused much hardship and distress among the hardy souls of East Texas. Farmers found themselves searching for new ways to support their families as they saw cotton prices fall and the boll weevil attack their crops. One answer came when President Roosevelt created programs designed to put Americans back to work. One of these programs was the Civilian Conservation Corps (CCC), which was a great success in East Texas and throughout the United States. Young, unemployed, unmarried men between the ages of 18 and 26 flocked to sign up for the program, which involved building schools, parks, roads, and bridges while living a military lifestyle. The local forestry companies and railroad companies also fell into financial difficulty, although they were the sole livelihood for many families.

Feeling restless from the tough economic times, many young Nacogdoches men joined the military to help support their families and to see the world. When Pearl Harbor was bombed, some local military men were on ships docked in the bay. Most of them were injured, but luckily, no Nacogdoches County men were killed that day. By early 1942, families from all over Nacogdoches County had sons in the war, and flags hung in their windows with blue stars for sons serving in the war and gold stars for sons who had died in the war. In 1943, the Nacogdoches Boosters Club honored 16 "Four Star Mothers," who had four or more sons serving in the military, with U.S. War Department medals. This was a great honor in the days of great patriotism. On January 24, 1942, Thomas Marvin Pitts, from the Alazan community, was the first man killed in action during the Battle of Bataan on the Philippine Islands; many more followed thereafter.

On the home front, judge Albert Warren "A. W." Bell, county judge, appealed to the public to turn to an all-out war effort and began preparing his county of 35,000 for a unified defense. Stephen F. Austin State Teachers College (SFASTC) joined the effort as enrollment dropped to an all-time low of 300 students. To tap into the national defense theme, SFASTC president Paul Boynton signed an agreement in 1943 with the U.S. War Department to bring the first Women's Army Corps training school to the campus. SFASTC also set up the Red Cross Motor Corps and the Civil Defense Corps. The Nacogdoches Council of Defense was formed to sell war bonds and rationing stamps, and the 44th Battalion of the Home Defense Guard established its six county headquarters in Nacogdoches. County schools joined in by having scrap metal drives and special training courses for the men about to go to war. According to a December 1941 issue of the *Daily Sentinel*, businesses like Cason, Monk & Company displayed defense windows showing that "two things must go hand and hand in 1942 to whip the Japs: buying of defense bonds and stamps and the planting and raising of more foodstuffs." Twelve days after the bombing of Pearl Harbor, the town had its first Friday night blackout in keeping with the desires of the Office of Civilian Defense and of Governor Stevenson.

By the end of December 1941, Congress had changed the minimum registration age from 20 to 18, making all men from 18 to 64 eligible for draft. Volunteers manned registration booths set up at various voting precincts on what was dubbed "R-Day" as thousands of young men from the city and far-reaching areas of the county came to register.

Patriotism ruled as men as young as 16 told recruiters they were 18 just to join the fight. Rich and poor, white and African American, young and old, male and female—they all signed up to do their part. From Alaska, the South Pacific, Germany, France, and North Africa, Nacogdoches men and women were all over the world. Many died; others were lost at sea, held for years as POWs, wounded, missing in action, died from disease, and surprisingly many died in training accidents or other accidents in war fields. If they were one of the lucky ones to return home, they came home more mature and ready to live the American dream. They took advantage of the GI Bill by going to college or trade school; they bought houses, got married, and had babies. To this day, if one talks to one of the ever-dwindling number of surviving veterans, they will readily say that they served in the greatest war the world has ever known, but the GI bill was the best thing that ever happened to them upon their return.

How many men did Nacogdoches County lose in the war? Surprisingly the number has never been tabulated. The list in this book contains more than 100 names and was compiled from the U.S. Army, Navy, Marine Corps, Coast Guard, and Merchant Marine lists available through the National Archives. In addition, names were obtained from Stephen F. Austin State University, Nacogdoches High School, archived copies of the *Daily Sentinel*, surrounding towns, neighbors, friends, funeral homes, and cemeteries. This list includes not only those who died as a direct result of enemy action, but also includes those unfortunate souls who died in captivity as prisoners of war, who were reported missing in action, who died from disease, and those who died stateside in training accidents, plane crashes, and other deaths while in military service. If a man left home to prepare for war and never returned due to death, he died in honor for his country and is a part of the list at the end of this book.

Over the years, some of these heroes readily told their war stories, but others remained silent and haunted by their memories. Regardless of how they chose to live their lives, no one will ever really know what they experienced at such a young age. These experiences created a special breed of men and women who have high moral standards and a deep love of country, like no other generation. Their era will soon pass and they will all be gone, leaving a legacy of true patriotism. Their memories will remain through stories and photographs, some of which are shared here.

One

The Great Depression Ends

The onset of World War II, and the events that followed, transformed Texas forever. Up until this time, most of the people of Nacogdoches County, like most Texans, still lived in rural farming communities. In 1939, sharecroppers like Frank "Jack" Molandes Jr. (above), still plowed cotton fields behind mules. The hard life on the farm readied the men for the hard years that followed. By early 1942, World War II had begun to draw hundreds of thousands of rural Texans into the military. (Courtesy of Lois Lazarine Molandes.)

During the Great Depression, lumbering in Texas found growth and expansion, even though prices were much lower than the early 1920s. In Nacogdoches County, Frost Johnson Lumber Company and hundreds of other sawmills in the county created a livelihood when no other work was available. The jobs were hard labor, dangerous, and the days were long, as the men followed the logging operations deep into remote areas of the county. (Courtesy of ETRC, SFASU.)

Commercial National Bank (CNB), organized in 1901, was hard hit by the sagging economy of the Great Depression. With high unemployment and depressed crop prices, farmers defaulted on their annual bank loans in great numbers. Under the watchful eye of president Thomas W. Baker, CNB was able to successfully weather the economic storm of the Depression and continues to serve the community today as Commercial Bank of Texas. (Courtesy of ETRC, SFASU.)

For the first time since 1921, the Nacogdoches High School (NHS) Dragon football team, in the fall of 1939, won a district championship. Undoubtedly this young team is one of the most memorable teams ever to walk the halls of 'Doches High and wear the gold and black. Quarterback Thomas Marion "Buddy" Hawkins (left) led his 24-man team to a rain-soaked, 8-6 win over Lufkin and took the championship that year. Before World War II was over, most of these young men went to war. Six lost their lives and never returned. They were Charles Lee "Sluefoot" Brantley, Fred Buckner, Frank Miller, Major "M. F." Russell, John "Little Rod" Rodrigues, and Loarn "Bull" Weems. In this photograph, Hawkins is shown with his best friend, Clinton Crisp. (Courtesy of Thomas Marion Hawkins.)

The Works Progress Administration (WPA), a New Deal program, was designed to put the youth of America to work during the Depression. Its mark is still seen all around town, as in the new high school on Mound Street built in 1939 at a cost of $350,000. The building is now Thomas J. Rusk Elementary School. The WPA also paved Main and North Streets with bricks, built several buildings at SFASTC, and began construction of a new airport in 1942. (Left, courtesy of Ruby Cortines King; below, courtesy of Joyce Bright Swearingen.)

The NHS class of 1940 consisted of 83 students and was the first graduating class in the new high school built by the WPA. In the spring of that year, working like ants, the students and janitors moved all the desks and chairs from the old Red Building to the new school. After the move, the old Red Building became the Central Grammar School. (Courtesy of Joyce Bright Swearingen.)

In the fall of 1941, the NHS Dragon district championship football team played "the game of the century" against Lufkin and won with a score of 7-6. The team consisted of, from left to right, (first row) L. O. Lindsey, Bill Garner, Roy Hanna, Dick Wright, John Wilson, Edwin Gaston, and Jim Wilson; (second row) Charles Beck, James Walters, Loarn Weems, Frank Sisco, T. C. Stephens, Howard Miller, and John Winder; (third row) coach Bryan Schely, Billy Nichols, Nelson Loveless, Junior Buckner, Buck Fausett, managers Hubert Mott, Charles Rymes, and William Bell, and coach Bill Echols. (Courtesy of NHS Alumni Association.)

The entire staff of the Cushing school district, for the school year ending May 1938, is pictured above. Superintendent Roy Self (back row, far right) kept records that state the entire budget for the school year was $23,930, including the salary for the bus drivers. Self was a well-known school administrator in the area, also serving as superintendent at Sacul, Woden, and Douglass. (Courtesy of Jan Dobbs Barton.)

Frost Johnson Lumber Company, located at Hayward and Butt Streets in Nacogdoches, was a self-contained sawmill town from 1904 to 1954. The company workers and their families lived in rented, company-owned housing, and bought their groceries and clothing from the company-owned store. The despair of the time is captured in the faces of the workers in this photograph taken July 1939. (Courtesy of the ETRC, SFASU.)

Two

The War Begins at Pearl Harbor

December 7, 1941, on a quiet Hawaiian Sunday morning at 7:40 a.m., 183 Japanese planes began their attack formation off the coast of Oahu. At 7:53 a.m., seeing the U.S. Pacific Fleet off guard, the pilots received the attack order, "Tora, Tora, Tora!" This aerial view of Battleship Row was photographed from a Japanese aircraft soon after the USS *Arizona* was bombed. The attack marked the beginning of World War II. (Courtesy of the National Archives.)

Frank Robert Cabiness (right), 26, of the U.S. Marines, was on the deck of the USS *Arizona* when she was bombed by the Japanese. The ship sank in nine minutes, trapping hundreds. The *Arizona* lost 1,177 men (over half of the casualties suffered by the entire fleet in the attack) and had 334 survivors, including Cabiness. Married to Ella Mae Ray of Nacogdoches, he is pictured here with his father, Tom. (Courtesy of Jerry Cabiness.)

Ralph Griffith, of the U.S. Navy, from Melrose, was aboard the USS *Raleigh*, docked at Ford Island, when the light cruiser was hit and badly damaged by a torpedo. Griffith was blown from the ship. His only memory was waking up while being transported to a Mare Island Naval Hospital in San Francisco Bay. (Courtesy of Bobby Johnson and ETRC, SFASU.)

Edsel "Dootsie" McIver (left), of the U.S. Navy, was aboard the USS *Oklahoma* when it was hit early in the attack on Pearl Harbor. As the ship sank, the crew was ordered overboard and 415 men were killed. Many others were injured, including Dootsie. Hearing the news of the attack on the other side of the island, Jerome McIver rushed to find his brother. He remembered seeing how fast the atmosphere went from a still, quiet, lush paradise to a hellish inferno. Dootsie earned 14 battle stars before he was killed in January 1945. Pictured with Dootsie is his older brother, Rex McIver (right), who was the second commander of VFW Post No. 3893 and who helped publish *The Men and Women in World War II from Nacogdoches County* in 1946. (Courtesy of Kirk McIver.)

J. B. Bullock graduated from high school at 16 and joined the U.S. Navy in 1940 because his parents did not have the money to send him to college and he wanted to see the world. At 18, he was an electrician aboard the USS *Nevada* when the Japanese attacked Pearl Harbor. He remembers it was a Sunday morning, and he was about to take a shower when he saw the first bomb drop. Bullock survived the attack and the rest of the war. He retired from the U.S. Navy in 1966. The USS *Nevada* is shown here beached and burning after being hit by Japanese bombs and torpedoes. Her pilothouse area is discolored by fires in that vicinity. (Left, courtesy of Mary Luna Bullock; below, courtesy of the National Archives.)

The USS *Northampton* steamed into Pearl Harbor on the morning of December 8, 1941, the day after the attack. The heavy cruiser had been at sea with Vice Adm. William "Bull" Halsey Jr.'s task force, escorting the USS *Hornet* to Midway. Aboard the cruiser was Cushing native George Self, 18, with the U.S. Navy, who remembers witnessing the devastation and seeing eight inches of oil floating on the water in the harbor. (Courtesy of George Self.)

Henry Arthur "Hank" Spies and his fiancée, Hazel Lee, decided to elope on Saturday, December 6, 1941. While on their way to Houston, they stopped in Cleveland and got married at the First Methodist Church. As soon as the wedding was over, the minister told them Pearl Harbor had been bombed. Soon afterwards, Hank joined the U.S. Navy Seabees. (Courtesy of Mildred Lee Pitts.)

SECOND Extra!

The Daily Sentinel

THE NEWSPAPER THAT SERVES THE NACOGDOCHES AREA

WAR DECLARED

JAP BOMBERS DROP DEATH ON PEARL HARBOR

NIPPON DECLARES WAR ON U.S. AND BRITAIN

BULLETIN

President Calls Congress To Act As Shooting Is Started

War with Japan became a reality Sunday by the declara- tion when Japanese airplanes attacked military bases on the is- land of Oahu, Hawaii, Manila and torpedoed an army transport 1300 miles west of San Francisco in the Pacific ocean in an all ou unprovoked and unheralded attack on United States military ob- jectives.

President Roosevelt immediately took steps to call Congress to meet in Washington at once to give consideration to further ac tion on the war that has now become a fact.

Reds Push Back Nazi Attacks on Mozhaisk Sector

Cousin of Local Man Shoots Down Four Axis Planes

FLASH

The Japanese government has announced a state of war with the United States.

S. S. Oklahoma Set Afire By Bombs

FRANKLIN D. ROOSEVELT

The *Daily Sentinel Extra* edition, dated Sunday, December 7, 1941, was handed out on the streets of Nacogdoches just a few hours after the bombing of Pearl Harbor. Although most people did not know the location of Pearl Harbor, they quickly learned that this event was the beginning of terrible times to come. War with Japan was inevitable! (Courtesy of the ETRC, the Annie Virginia Sanders Collection, and the *Daily Sentinel*.)

In the same *Daily Sentinel Extra* (above), Royal Air Force (RAF) pilot Lance Wade is reported shooting down four enemy fighters over Libya on his 27th birthday. He became one of the highest-scoring RAF American "flying aces" in World War II. He died in an accidental plane crash in January 1944 in Foggia, Italy. Inducted into Texas Aviation Hall of Fame in 2005, he is buried at the McKnight Cemetery. (Courtesy of ETRC, SFASU.)

Hazel Shelton Abernethy, 14, was a sophomore at NHS on December 7, 1941, the day Pearl Harbor was bombed. She remembers being at the Stone Fort Theatre with a group of friends watching the movie *Till We Meet Again*. When she came out of the theatre at about 4:30 p.m., the *Daily Sentinel Extra* was being sold. It announced, "Jap Bombers Drop Death on Pearl Harbor." (Courtesy of Nacogdoches High School Alumni Association.)

On Friday night before Pearl Harbor was bombed, the Nacogdoches Dragons played a bi-district game against Tyler. The Stone Fort Theatre, located downtown on the square, enticed the team to win with a free pass to see "Jarrin'" John Jimbrough in the movie *Lone Star Ranger*. They lost that game, but because of their district title, they were allowed see the movie on Monday, the day after the Pearl Harbor attack. (Courtesy of Linda Greer.)

Alton William "A. W." Birdwell, president of SFASTC when the war broke out, was troubled by the war. Early in 1942, he wrote in the *Stone Fort* yearbook, "The whole world is being tried by fire. Character, courage, endurance, religion are being tested as never before. " Later that year, he retired and was replaced as president by Dr. Paul Boynton, a George Peabody College master's graduate. (Courtesy of ETRC, SFASU.)

On December 8, 1941, Robert Wynne "Bob" Murphey, president of the student body, and A. W. Birdwell, president of SFASTC, armed with an old standup radio, gathered the SFASTC students in the auditorium to listen to President Roosevelt's Infamy speech to a joint session of Congress. (Courtesy of Reba Jane Gayler.)

Joyce Bright Swearingen and her husband, Doug Swearingen, both students at SFASTC when Pearl Harbor was bombed, married after the war in 1946. The day after Pearl Harbor was bombed, Joyce remembers gathering in the auditorium at SFASTC to listen to President Roosevelt's Infamy speech to a joint Congress. Her opinion was that the students entered the auditorium young and carefree and exited with their lives changed forever. Doug was the editor of the *Stone Fort*, SFASTC's yearbook, from 1941 to 1942. He graduated from SFASTC in 1942 and taught one year before he was drafted into the U.S. Army Air Corps in March 1943. (Courtesy of Joyce Bright Swearingen.)

Immediately after the attack on Pearl Harbor, Nacogdoches County judge Albert Warren "A. W." Bell (left, with his wife, Sallie Green) went into emergency response mode. He immediately appealed to the public to "turn to an all out war effort" and urged local residents and students "to do our work better than we ever have before." Bell was a three-term Nacogdoches county judge. (Courtesy of Susie Bell Wiggins.)

For the family of Claude Knox in Woden, sorrow turned to overwhelming joy on Christmas Eve 1941 when a letter arrived from him in Hawaii dated December 17. A few days earlier, they had received a letter from the U.S. Navy advising them that he had been killed in action at Pearl Harbor while on the USS *California*. (Courtesy of Kristin Knox Paradis.)

Three

Nacogdoches County Does Business

Novell Bright Modern Grocery, "the Home of Good Food," operated 39 years before closing on September 3, 1945. The store struggled during the war due to rationing and the fact that 20 of its clerks were called to duty to fight for their country. Lonnie Stone, a 21-year employee, and others went to work for the new store, B&C Grocery. (Courtesy of Joyce Bright Swearingen.)

The farmers market by the railroad tracks was a place for farmers to bring their fresh, locally grown crops to sell to the general public or to ship to other states via the railroad. In this photograph, farmers brought watermelons to sell. The watermelons were then loaded in freight cars and shipped to different parts of the United States. (Courtesy of ETRC, SFASU.)

Hunt Plumbing Supply Company, located next door to the Farmers Supply Company, under the leadership of Lawrence Crawford Hunt, grew into a multimillion dollar enterprise by the end of the war. It operated as a wholesale plumbing supply house. (Courtesy of ETRC, SFASU.)

Texas Farm Products Company, organized by M. S. Wright Sr., was formed on January 15, 1930, to bring fertilizer to the East Texas farmer. In 1942, Wright bought all outstanding shares in the company and it became a family-owned business. Always supportive of the war effort, and successful from the beginning, the company now sells its products all over the world. (Courtesy of ETRC, SFASU.)

When the war began, Cason Monk Funeral Home, located on Mound Street across from the new high school, had recently merged with Branch Patton Funeral Home. Also in town were Oakley Metcalf Funeral Home and Sid Roberts Funeral Home. Beginning in 1947, it was to these funeral homes that the majority of the Nacogdoches casualties of war were brought. (Courtesy Sue Fogle.)

In 1942, the U.S. Navy's demand for ships and the Nacogdoches Chamber of Commerce's offer to provide 5 acres of prime real estate influenced Northern Indiana Brass Foundry Company's (NIBCO) decision to build a manufacturing plant in Nacogdoches. The new plant opened in 1942 with 32 employees, all former farmers, loggers, and sawmill workers. The plant produced bronze valves for naval vessels, including destroyers, cruisers, battleships, and submarines. A U.S. Navy inspector was on sight at all times to observe each valve as it was tested. In addition to the ship valves, NIBCO also produced cast and wrought iron fittings for airplanes, as is indicated by the "Keep 'em Flying" war advertisement (left), which appeared in *Domestic Engineering* magazine in January 1942. (Both courtesy of NIBCO, Inc.)

The Nacogdoches Post Office, the center of the square in downtown Nacogdoches, was a popular place for letters going to and coming from soldiers in the war. It was also the site of sadness when a Western Union telegram came from the U.S. War Department announcing the death of a soldier. (Courtesy of ETRC, SFASU.)

The Nacogdoches County Courthouse, built in 1912, was called an "ugly monstrosity" by 1946 county judge Grady Fuller. That year, the American Legion and the Veterans of Foreign Wars began petitioning for a memorial courthouse to serve as a meeting place for county veterans organizations. In 1959, a new courthouse was dedicated and it still serves the county after many renovations and additions. (Photograph by J. Griffis Smith; courtesy of Texas Highways.)

Lea's Bargain Store, next to the Redland Hotel, was closed after its owner, Pvt. John Aubrey Lea, 34, was killed in Ahrweiler, Germany, on March 7, 1945. He left a wife, Bessie McDonald, and three sons. His remains were brought home in December 1947 and he was buried in the Greenwood Cemetery in Harrison County. (Courtesy of ETRC, SFASU.)

Specializing in first-class repair service for all makes of cars and trucks, Ben T. Wilson Chevrolet Company, located downtown on the square, advertised, "Our Job . . . To keep them rolling for Victory!" Repair was emphasized because the sale of private automobiles was prohibited by the Office of Price Administration beginning in 1942. (Courtesy of Mildred Lee Pitts.)

The Airline Motor Coaches of East Texas was a vital aspect of transportation during the war. When tires and gas were rationed, the bus line experienced a boom. It was not unusual to have 90 to 100 passengers filling 37 bus seats. The company was founded in 1930 by C. D. Thomas Sr. and was sold after the war for $1.5 million. Brothers Oswald (sixth from left) and Leonell (kneeling, far right) Scarborough, who both served in the military during World War II, are pictured here with the other employees of the company. (Courtesy of Leonette Scarborough Thomas.)

The *Daily Sentinel* newspaper was published in the Herald Building located on North Fredonia, across from the Airline Bus Company. During the war, John VanCronkite, editor in 1945, had the grim responsibility of reporting the news, which often included news of young men who were missing in action, wounded, and had died. Their slogan was, "Truth, Justice and Right." (Courtesy of ETRC, SFASU.)

Joyce Bright (left) stands with Jimmy Dorsey (center) and Brownie Jo Patton (right) on the sign at the front entrance to the Piney Woods Country Club on Highway 59 South. The country club, under the direction of new president M. S. "Skinny" Garrison, in 1945, expanded their nine hole golf course to a modern 18-hole course. (Courtesy of Joyce Bright Swearingen.)

Like today, many businesses during the war were dependent on the college trade. Two of these businesses were Jordan's Café and Jordan's Beauty Shop, located on South Street. In 1943, SFASU's *Stone Fort Yearbook* advertised Jordan's as, "Where the Students Go." The building still stands on South Street and is now the home of Nuevo Look Hair Salon. (Courtesy of ETRC, SFASU.)

Four

STEPHEN F. AUSTIN TEACHERS COLLEGE ADAPTS TO WAR

To adapt to the war changes after Pearl Harbor, SFASTC shifted its attention from training teachers to an all-out effort of preparing its students for war and to the protection of the home front. To add to the tough times, their first and only president, Dr. A. W. Birdwell, decided to retire in the fall of 1941. He was replaced by Dr. Paul Boynton. (Courtesy of ETRC, SFASU.)

The SFASTC football team (above), in the fall of 1941, was the last team for the duration of the war. That year, coach Maurice "M. A." Baumgarten played the fall season with rookie freshmen and sophomores because the older athletes had been called to service. At the end of the season, intercollegiate football, along with tennis and golf, were curtailed. By the end of 1942, both Baumgarten (below, right) and his assistant coach Ralph Murph (below, left) had both been called to service to the U.S. Naval Reserves. (Both courtesy ETRC, SFASU.)

Intercollegiate basketball continued under the direction of Stanford McKewen, although football had been discontinued. McKewen had replaced former coach Robert "Bob" Shelton and later became SFASTC's registrar. Pictured here is the fall 1942 SFASTC basketball team with Coach Shelton. (Courtesy of ETRC, SFASU.)

Intramural sports were strongly emphasized in 1943, along with physical fitness. Pictured here are, from left to right, U.S. Marine Reserve champions Charles Kilpatrick, Purvis Lowery, Ray Tarrant, Mylrea "Chigger" Berry, James Howard Milstead, Dayton Carter, and Edwin Gaston. Enlisted reserves from the U.S. Army, Marines, Army Air Corps, Navy Air Corps, and Navy participated in the competition. (Courtesy of ETRC, SFASU.)

Instead of football, golf, and tennis, SFASTC implemented a rigorous calisthenics course to prepare the men for the physical needs of the armed forces. The course used the U.S. Navy method of training. (Courtesy of ETRC, SFASU.)

The last play for the duration of the war was presented at SFASTC on November 19, 1943, under the direction of Burney Howard, head of the speech and drama department. Howard took a leave of absence later that year when he was drafted into the armed forces. In the photograph above, Douglas Swearingen (sixth from left) is an actor in the play *Ceiling Zero* performed in 1941. (Courtesy of Joyce Bright Swearingen.)

The Grand Order of the Royal Barristers was a pre-law club at the college. Here members are seated in front of the World War II banner made by Ellen H. Richard's homemaking class in 1942. The flag had a blue star for every SFASTC soldier in service and gold stars for every soldier who had died in service for his country. The flag hung in the recreation room of the Austin Building for the duration of the war. (Courtesy of Edward Abernethy.)

The members of the Sawyers, the oldest boys club at SFASTC, all went to war. Pictured are, from left to right (first row) B. E. Howard, Lester Smith, Charles Ruth, Johnny Brittain, Lon Tullos, Don Barkett, Billy Fleetwood, Louis Collida, and Douglas Swearingen; (second row) Roy Walley, Sherrod Caborne, Kurl Shirey, Charles Brittain, Percy Plount, O. E. Permenter, Gene Currington, Ray Tuggle, and Autrey Maddox; (third row) Bobby Clifford, Joe Henson, Wade Clendenen, Lavoy Moore, Mitchell Jetton, Orville Todd, Ray Die, Pat Nash, David Trice, Tom Sharpe, and C. D. Thomas. (Courtesy of ETRC, SFASU.)

Before the war, SFASTC's sorority the Pine Burrs knitted Bundles for Britain but diverted their knitting skills to aid U.S. soldiers when the war began. Some of the prominent ladies who were members of the sorority and pictured here are Lucas Kingham, Joyce Bright Swearingen, Alma Stallings Brittain, Jo Anna Loden Bentley, Joy Bell Die, Fairy Brown Nash, Tommye Earle Beach Adams, Margie Partin Kilpatarick, Linda Langston Due, and Edel Zeve. (Courtesy of Joyce Bright Swearingen.)

The four Stone Fort beauty queen candidates were, from left to right, Barbara Perkins, Nacogdoches; Judy King, Mount Enterprise; Beth Drennen, Kilgore; and Pricilla Burns, Troup. The queen, Barbara Perkins, was selected by 4,000 U.S. Naval cadets at the Corpus Christi Naval Air Center on May 2, 1943. Due to wartime difficulties that year, the queen's ball was cancelled. (Official U.S. Navy Photograph.)

In 1943, SFASTC band director J. T. Cox enlisted women and demonstration school students to perform in the first all-girl band. The band was unable to travel, due to rationing of gasoline and tires, so they mostly performed at local events. In addition, their band hall was converted to barracks for the headquarters of the local WAC school. (Courtesy of Edward Abernethy.)

Pres. Paul Boynton allowed the SFASTC library to become a regional depository for donated books. Under this program, the library staff sorted and packaged the books, then shipped them to special centers across the nation. From the centers, they were shipped to servicemen, who always looked forward to receiving mail from home. (Courtesy of ETRC, SFASU.)

Pres. Paul Boynton is credited with saving SFASTC during the war, when the enrollment dropped from 900 to 300 in the fall of 1942. Struggling with what to do about the declining enrollment, he asked the board of regents to allow him to go to Washington, D.C., to petition the War Manpower Commission for a new training school for women. His proposal was accepted and the Army Administration School, WAC No. 1 came to Nacogdoches in 1943. (Courtesy of ETRC, SFASU.)

Life went on at SFASTC, although the war raged. This photograph, taken in the spring of 1943, shows the class favorites, who are, from left to right (first row), Alma Houston Stallings, Joyce Bright Swearingen, and Charles Kilpatrick; (second row) Marie Kenley Shirey, Charles Keith Ruth, Mitchell Jetton, Linda Langston, and Charles Runnels. Runnels is currently the chancellor emeritus of Pepperdine University in Malibu, California. (Courtesy of Joyce Bright Swearingen.)

In December 1944, the 2,560-acre SFA Experimental Forest (SFAEF) was established and became the first in the nation. Under the leadership of Dr. Boynton, it played a key factor in the establishment of the SFASTC's Department of Forestry. In 1945, curriculum and classes were established so the first forestry classes would be available to the returning veterans in the spring of 1946. (Courtesy of U.S. Forestry Service [USFS].)

Chireno native William Bernard "Bill" Duke, 26, had a college degree in agriculture when he joined the U.S. Army Air Corps in December 1941. After being discharged in October 1945, and after helping his family make their annual molasses, he became the first SFAEF forest technician in November 1945. Duke, along with his dedicated employees—Vic Pena, Frank Manchaca, and Rene Alcaniz—made the SFAEF an excellent research and educational facility. (Courtesy of Ruby Duke.)

SFASTC contributed two American Red Cross units to aid in the civil defense of the city and county. The units were made up of college students and faculty volunteers who maintained casualty stations at the Redland and Liberty Hotels. The new high school served as an emergency field hospital. In this photograph, the sign in front of the Rusk Building reads, "Central First Aid Station." (Courtesy of ETRC, SFASU.)

On May 25, 1942, Dr. Sidney Garrison, president of George Peabody College for Teachers, delivered the commencement address for 112 graduates of the draft-riddled senior class. By the end of that summer, most of the men in the class had been drafted, trained, and were ready to depart for foreign lands. Through the duration of the war, SFASTC lost 36 former students. (Courtesy of ETRC, SFASU.)

Five

The Women's Army Corps Marches into Town

The U.S. Army Administration's Women's Army Corps "WAC" Branch No. 1 opened at SFASTC on February 15, 1943, at a time when enrollment had dropped below 900 students. The WAC unit was the first of its kind in the nation. This photograph of the "Army Administration School Personnel Only" sign was taken in front of the Rusk Building. (Courtesy of ETRC, SFASU.)

On Friday, February 12, 1943, at 2 p.m., 250 uniformed WACs stepped off the Southern Pacific train at the train depot. They were led by the college band through downtown and up Mound Street to their dormitories. This photograph is of Company A arriving at the train depot. They were the first detachment of its kind and had just completed a three-week basic training course in Des Moines, Iowa. The purpose of the school was to make available to the national defense the knowledge, skill, and special training of the women of the nation. (Both courtesy of ETRC, SFASU.)

The women who entered the WAC training school came from all walks of life. Applicants had to be U.S. citizens between the ages of 21 and 44, have no dependents, be at least five feet tall and in good health, and weigh 100 pounds or more. Beginning pay was $54 a month, the same as a U.S. Army enlisted man. (Courtesy of ETRC, SFASU.)

This photograph was taken as the women of Company A marched to the mess hall for the first time on February 12, 1943. The six-week training courses overlapped as new classes started every three weeks. Approximately 600 recruits were on campus at all times. For this reason, college students were housed in private homes and off-campus apartments. (Courtesy of ETRC, SFASU.)

Wisely Hall and Gibbs Hall served as the dormitories for the women enrolled in the WAC program. In this photograph, the women wait at Gibbs Hall for entrance into their dormitories. First wakeup call was at 6 a.m. every morning, six days a week. Lights were out five days a week at 10:30 p.m. and midnight on Saturday and Sunday. (Courtesy of ETRC, SFASU.)

About 50 enlisted and commissioned personnel and civilians were assigned to training duties on a permanent basis. This photograph, taken September 29, 1943, is of an instructors meeting held by Capt. Ellen M. Bailey (far left) from Houston, Texas. (Courtesy of ETRC, SFASU.)

The majority of the coursework for the auxiliaries focused on administrative training. They learned everything necessary to be stenographers, typists, translators, legal secretaries, cryptographers, telegraph and teletype operators, radiographers, general clerks, and much more. Their curriculum included 87 courses taken over a six-week period. Classes were held seven hours a day, plus one-hour of drills. (Courtesy of ETRC, SFASU.)

Shown in this photograph changing a tire on a U.S. Army truck are Auxiliary First Class Gladys Knowles (left) and Auxiliary First Class Thelma Graff (right). By the time the school closed in March 1944, about 3,000 women had trained at SFASTC. (Courtesy of ETRC, SFASU.)

Smiling for the Signal Corps photographer is Vivian O'Rourke of Chicago, Illinois. She was engaged in a motor transport class when this photograph was taken. After training, the auxiliaries were sent throughout the nation and abroad to do their jobs. (Courtesy of ETRC, SFASU.)

Permanent Headquarters Company were assigned duties as mail clerks, correspondence clerks, payroll clerks, chauffeurs, truck drivers, and nurses, among others. Receiving mail from family and friends was always a joyous time for the ladies. The Post Exchange was located in the Women's Recreation Center. (Courtesy of ETRC, SFASU.)

A strict dress code was adhered to at all times. As shown here, the ladies were required to wear dresses during physical training. They are seen here in a volleyball game on September 26, 1943. The only time they could wear civilian clothing was for a half-day on Saturday and all day Sunday. A moderate amount of makeup was allowed. (Courtesy of ETRC, SFASU.)

The WACs were visible all around town. They attended churches, made speeches for local organizations, and frequently socialized with the local young men and women. This photograph, taken by Norvell Pitts in 1943, is of three young WACs in front of the La Casa Piedra, known as the Old Stone Fort, which was built by the Spanish in 1779 as the first mercantile house in Nacogdoches. (Courtesy of Mildred Pitts.)

The graduation exercise for Class No. 1, WAC Branch No. 1 of the Army Administration School was held on March 24, 1943, in the Nacogdoches High School auditorium. Brig. Gen. Herbert C. Holdridge is shown greeting Auxiliary First Class Faye Johannesen. She was graduate No. 1 of class No. 1. (Courtesy of ETRC, SFASU.)

Mary Prado (center), daughter of Thomas and Kathleen Prado of Nacogdoches, stands with two friends at Camp Kilmer, New Jersey. She was recruited into the WACs in 1944 and was assigned to Camp Kilmer near New Brunswick, New Jersey. She met George Muzyczka, also in the U.S. Army, in New Jersey, and they were married in June 1948. (Courtesy of Jane Prado Luna.)

Six

The Nazis Arrive in East Texas

In early 1944, the War Manpower Commission established POW Camp Chireno as a permanent branch of Camp Fannin in Smith County. Camp Chireno was located on 30 acres of leased land, west of Chireno on the Chireno-Etoile road. It received the first 300 German POWs in May 1944 for the purpose of cutting and salvaging timber damaged by a severe ice storm earlier in the year. (Courtesy of Chireno Historical Society.)

One of the worst ice storms recorded in the history of East Texas occurred in January 1944. The heavy sleet and the howling winds caused a dangerous buildup of ice on the vast forests in and around Nacogdoches County. The limbs of the trees, loaded with ice, caused heavy damage to thousands of trees, especially the native pine trees. Not wanting to lose the precious timber, Frost Johnson Lumber Company in Nacogdoches (below) and Angelina County Lumber Company in Lufkin received permission from the War Manpower Commission to establish Camp Chireno. The camp was built in less than a month and received its first prisoners in May 1944. (Both courtesy of ETRC, SFASU.)

The German POWs at Camp Chireno were from Rommel's Afrika Korps captured in North Africa in 1943. More than 425,000 enemy POWs were sent to U.S. camps during World War II because it was less burdensome and costly to house and feed them in America. This photograph is of a group of POWs held at Camp 72 in Ludwigsburg, Germany, in 1945. (Photograph by John Jack Forman, courtesy of ETRC, SFASU.)

Sgt. Tony Ball (right) at nearby Camp San Augustine is shown with a German POW. The eight-prisoner, pyramidal tents in the background were common at all camps, including Camp Chireno. (Courtesy of ETRC, SFASU.)

Sgt. George Goetz, behind the wheel, and an unidentified guard at Camp San Augustine are shown with the Friedrich Keidel family home in the background. One of the Keidel daughters fell in love with a POW and they later married. (Courtesy of ETRC, SFASU.)

Two German POWS are pictured here sawing logs on lumber company land. They cut and trimmed the logs to required lengths: 4-feet for pulpwood and 12- and 18-feet for lumber. (Courtesy of the National Archives.)

After the lumber was cut and trimmed, prisoners would load a mule team with pulpwood logs from the stacks. The logs were then pulled by the team of mules to a central location on the logging road where they were piled for collection by a company truck. These photographs were taken by the U.S. Army Signal Corps on November 20, 1944. (Courtesy of the National Archives.)

This photograph was taken in the Trawick Yard in northwest Nacogdoches County on November 20, 1944, by the U.S. Army Signal Corps. In this lumberyard, there were 26 POWs consisting of 25 workers and one corporal. The prisoners loaded four freight cars simultaneously, then the wood was shipped to the mills in Nacogdoches and Lufkin. (Courtesy of the National Archives.)

At the lumber mills, the wood was trimmed and faced into boards. Then they were dried and stacked in the yard for shipment. These prisoners are working at Zeagler Lumber Company in Lufkin, Texas. The letters "PW" were worn on the clothing of all the Germans prisoners. This photograph was taken by the U.S. Army Signal Corps on November 20, 1944. (Courtesy of the National Archives.)

At the end of a day's work, the prisoners would do all necessary work to get ready for the next day. Here two POWs are filing and sharpening the handsaws. This photograph was taken by the U.S. Army Signal Corps on November 20, 1944. (Courtesy of the National Archives.)

In the photograph taken at Camp San Augustine, Sgt. Tony Ball (left) is shown standing next to a prison guard. It was rare that prisoners escaped, but when they did Merryman "M. C." Roebuck from Nacogdoches was called to bring his bloodhounds. In this case, the four escaped prisoners were captured the next day. Roebuck later became police chief in Nacogdoches. (Courtesy of ETRC, SFASU.)

U.S. Army personnel escort German inspection officers on a tour of a POW camp. The German POWs were treated so well that animosity existed in the general public. Often the camps were referred to as the "Fritz Ritz" because the POWs ate well and were paid 80¢ a day for their work; they even enjoyed radio programs and newspapers from their homelands. (Courtesy of the National Archives.)

In stark contrast to the Nazi prisoners' treatment in East Texas, the treatment of Americans held by Germans as POWs was considered harsh. Pfc. Richard Arriola, 24, was a medic with the 60th Infantry Regiment, 9th Infantry Division, when he was captured by Germans on February 4, 1945. Years later, he remembered being hungry all of the time. He said that once they found a dead horse on a roadside, so they cooked and ate it. (Courtesy of Jan Dobbs Barton.)

Sgt. Berdine Adams of Nacogdoches was a prisoner of war from 1942 to 1945. He was held at the Fukuoka No. 17 camp situated on the bay of Omuta, Japan, for more than two years. Rumors abounded in the camp that when an American invasion of Japan occurred all prisoners would be killed immediately. Adams was liberated on September 2, 1945. (Courtesy of Frank Adams.)

Pvt. Amon Blair (right), of Appleby, entered the U.S. Army in September 1941 and was with the 7th Army Chemical Company stationed in the Philippines at Baatan. On April 9, 1942, the Filipino-American forces at Bataan surrendered to the Japanese, and Blair became part of the infamous Bataan death march. He survived the march and spent two years in the Pasay prison before being loaded on the Japanese *Arisan Maru*, a "hell ship," to be transported to Japan. Not knowing the prisoners were aboard, the American submarine USS *Shark* torpedoed the ship on October 24, 1944. Of the 1,800 prisoners aboard, 1,795 died including Blair. (Courtesy of SFA Alumni Association.)

S.Sgt. Wilfred Gene Whitaker, of Cushing, also died on the Japanese *Arisan Maru*. He had entered the U.S. Army and was serving as a military policeman with the 808th Military Police Company in the Philippines when captured by the Japanese. He spent two years in the Cabanatuan Prison before he was put onto the Japanese *Arisan Maru* on October 24, 1944, which ultimately led to his death. We will never know if Blair and Whitaker met while onboard and discovered they were both from Nacogdoches. (Courtesy of SFA Alumni Association.)

On May 6, 1942, Pvt. John Triana (left), 19, with the 60th Coastal Artillery Regiment, and Cpl. Thomas Crawford (below), 24, with the 59th Coastal Artillery Regiment, were taken as Japanese POWs at Corregidor in the Philippines. They survived two years in captivity before being transported to Japan to perform slave labor for the Japanese. Both were freed in January 1945 in what became known as The Great Raid. Crawford's photograph taken just after his liberation is particularly striking in contrast to the photograph taken early in his enlistment. (Left, courtesy of Linda Triana Tyler; below, courtesy of Maurine Crawford Burkhalter.)

Seven

Schools and Churches Pray for Peace

The citizens of Nacogdoches, many of them with tears in their eyes, poured into churches all over town before dawn on June 6, 1944. They had awakened to sirens at 3 a.m. as police cars and ambulances roamed the streets announcing the beginning of the D-Day invasion. At Sacred Heart Catholic Church, the priest immediately said a Mass to pray that God would protect the men invading Hitler's occupied France. (Courtesy of Sacred Heart Catholic Church.)

First Baptist Church (above), together with Christ Episcopal Church, Sacred Heart Catholic Church, First Methodist Church, Grace Church, First Christian Church, Westminster Presbyterian Church, Assembly of God Church, and all other Nacogdoches churches held services and remained open throughout D-Day to allow members to gather for prayer. (Courtesy of ETRC, SFASU.)

Baptism in the river was a common custom in rural churches. In 1945, members of Bonaldo Baptist Church, in the Eden community, wait for immersion in the Angelina River. Jean Molandes Trautwein is shown minutes before her baptism. Her uncle Jessie Molandes' wife, Annie Manchack Molandes, awaits her turn. (Courtesy of Velma Molandes Miller.)

This group photograph was taken at the consecration of Christ Episcopal Church on May 12, 1940, at its third location on the corner of Mound Street and East Starr Avenue. Rev. Clinton Simon Quin, bishop of the Episcopal Diocese of Texas, stands in the center of the photograph with Rev. Orin Helvey, rector, to his right side. The church was founded in Nacogdoches in 1848. (Courtesy of ETRC, SFASU.)

Under the direction of Rev. Denis Monahan, members of the Catholic community at Moral gather in front of their new church, which was blessed by Bishop Christopher Edward Byrne on Easter Sunday, April 5, 1942. Three men from the parish died in service for their country during World War II: Bill Arriola, Floyd Rodrigues, and John Rodrigues. (Courtesy of Peggy Arriola Jasso.)

Rev. Emmett Hillary Mayes of First Methodist Church called his congregation to prayer at 4 a.m. on the morning of June 6, 1944. The D-Day services were held in their historic church built in 1910. Reverend Mayes was appointed minister of the church only one month before Pearl Harbor was bombed. (Courtesy of the First Methodist Church.)

The First Methodist Church formed the J. H. Hinds Sunday school class in February 1939. It was named after its founder, Capt. James Herbert Hinds, who was dean of the agriculture department at SFASTC. Hinds died in England at age 50 from complications arising from a crude surgery performed on him while he was serving in World War I. He died on June 4, 1944, and is buried at the Cambridge American Cemetery in Cambridge, England. (Courtesy of ETRC, SFASU.)

The Westminster Presbyterian Church has been "fulfilling God's mission" at its location at the corner of North Street and Powers Street since 1930, but the Presbyterian influence in Nacogdoches dates back to the 1830s. On D-Day, the church held predawn services where big crowds gathered. The church, under the direction of Rev. William F. Rogan, pastor, remained open all day. (Courtesy of Leonette Scarborough Thomas.)

In 1879, the Rev. Lawson Reed organized the Zion Hill Baptist Church, the first Baptist church serving the African American community in Nacogdoches. Reed, who died in 1924, is credited with the founding of 55 Baptist churches in the East Texas area. He was the grandfather of Clarence "Bo" McMichael who served proudly in the all "colored" 777th Field Artillery Battalion in Europe during the war. (Courtesy of Brian Bray.)

The youth program of First Christian Church was founded in 1920 and called the Christian Endeavor Society. During the height of the war, the pastor of the church, Rev. Charles Carrico, and the youth group, published a monthly newsletter called the *Beam* for servicemen. The staff members were Tommye Earle Beach, Imogene Maroney, Anna Lilla Moorer, Louise and Kate Marie Meador, Margie Hartsfield, and Joyce Bright. (Courtesy of Joyce Bright Swearingen.)

The Eden School represented many of the common schools in Nacogdoches County during the war years. It was a two-room, frame building with two teachers. Kids walked to school, discipline was strict, lunch was brought in a syrup bucket, and the school maintained a very positive influence in the community. When county schools were forced to close due to lack of funds, Eden became a part of the Douglass school system. (Courtesy of Edward Smith.)

Demonstration school student council members in 1943 are, from left to right, (first row) Joyce Brookshire, Helen Williams, Dannie Boone, and Dorothy Moore, all from the eleventh grade; Mary Beth Thompson, eighth grade; and Nelwyn Graves, tenth grade; (second row) Frank Touchstone, tenth grade; Charles Cooper, president; Doyle Turner and George Donald Feazell, ninth grade; Anne Yardley, sponsor; and Billy Byrd, ninth grade. (Courtesy of ETRC, SFASU.)

Thomas J. Rusk Junior High proudly flew a U.S. Treasury service flag because 94.83 percent of their class purchased war bonds in 1943. Shown here is the 1944 class student council. They are, from left to right, Sarah Ann Stone, Margie Nell Cole, Ruth Maynard, Bonnie Ruth Owens, Ed Morgan, faculty advisor F. A. Beall, Mildred Grimes, Edward Tucker, Johnny Rudisill, Grady Stallings, Thomas McGee, and Mary Frances Hardeman. (Courtesy of NHS Alumni Association.)

In January 1943, NHS added five new special war courses prescribed by the U.S. War Department. The courses were electricity, machines, shop, automobile mechanics, and radio. Pictured in this photograph from 1943 are student council officers, from left to right, vice president Billy Byrd, secretary Jeannine Jasper, advisor C. K. Chamberlain (acting superintendent of NHS), president Loy Reid, and sponsor Dora Grant. (Courtesy NHS Alumni Association.)

On October 11, 1944, a going-away party was given for U.S. Marine Charles Kimmey. NHS students pictured are, from left to right, (first row) Travis Shoup, Charlie Morgan, Charles Kimmey, Margie Hartsfield, Oliver Talmadge, Charlotte Perkins, and Janice Nicholson; (second row) Mary Kimmey, Jimmy Dorsey, Bobby Ellington, Carolyn Muckleroy, Charlie Mack Bailey, Helen Jean Buckner, Hazel Shelton, and Mary Elizabeth Talmadge; (third row) Jeanette Bailey, Dorothy Shelton, Betty Kimmey, Patricia Talmadge, Mary Jean McKinney, LaJeanne Hobson, and Mary Alice Tucker. (Courtesy NHS Alumni Association.)

Eight

The Home Front Does Its Part

The Headquarters Company of the 44th Battalion of the Texas Defense Guard was located in Nacogdoches. Company locations were Company A, Lufkin; Company B, Nacogdoches; Company C, Woodville; Company E, Hemphill; and Company F, Corrigan. Their mission was to take over the role of local defense when the U.S. National Guard was called to active duty. The captains of the companies are shown in this photograph. (Courtesy of Edward Abernethy.)

This photograph was taken on December 9, 1943, during a federal inspection of the Headquarters Company and Company B of the 44th Battalion of the Texas Defense Guard. In this photograph, from left to right, are 1st Lt. Edward Mueller, Capt. Reuel Tompkins, battalion commander Maj. Weldon Gilchrist, commanding officer of Company B Capt. Robert Shelton, and 1st Lt. Dewey Patterson, Company B. (Courtesy of Texas State Library and Archives Commission.)

Red Cross training was held in communities all over the county. The purpose was to establish local emergency care, since most of the doctors and nurses had gone into the armed forces. The Red Cross volunteers learned basic medical care and treatment. In this photograph, nurses are shown with their recently earned Red Cross certificates. (Courtesy of ETRC, SFASU.)

The Nacogdoches Boosters Club was organized in 1921 with the primary goals of cleaning up and beautifying Nacogdoches, boosting Stephen F. Austin College, improving the streets, and providing other services to the people. However, during the war they turned their attention to the families of the soldiers at war. In 1944, the club members recognized "Four Star Mothers" for having four or more sons in service. (Courtesy of ETRC, SFASU.)

Four Star Mothers were given medals and small flags to hang in their windows. The flags had blue stars for family members serving in the armed forces and gold stars for those loved ones who had died in service for their country. (Courtesy of Barbara Cason Merlie.)

James Elbert Reese, an active community leader, was the general chairman of the Nacogdoches County War and Community Chest Campaign. The countywide goal was $16,000 for 17 war chest agencies, including the Boy Scouts of America and the local Welfare Association. Reese's comment on this combined goal was, "At first the quota sounds a little high." (Courtesy of ETRC, SFASU.)

The wives of Rotary members were called Rotary Anns. Shown in this photograph, at a Rotary convention, are Nacogdoches Rotary Anns and their husbands. During the war, the Rotary Anns were very active selling war bonds, working in hospitals, and assisting the local ration board. They sold bonds from a booth set up on the sidewalk in front of McCrory's on Main Street. (Courtesy of ETRC, SFASU.)

When a soldier came home for leave, he was given special treatment by all his friends back home. They all knew that when he returned to service he may not come home again. Pictured here are, from left to right, Barbara Perkins Paine, Joyce Bright Swearingen, Lt. James Trimbel, Johnnie Partin Spies, and Margie Partin Kilpatrick. (Courtesy of Joyce Bright Swearingen.)

Dovie Bailey Bright was a volunteer Red Cross nurse during World War II. She and the other volunteers met at the Old Stone Fort to make bandages to be sent to soldiers. Later they had a special room designated as the Red Cross Room on the north side of the new high school building. In a good week they made more than 6,000 dressing bandages. (Courtesy of Joyce Bright Swearingen.)

The Ladies Altar Society of the Sacred Heart Church was very active in the day-to-day activities of the church. The women took care of the altars, cleaned the church, laundered and ironed the linens and gave the rectory a regular cleaning. Pictured here in 1940 are the ladies of the Altar Society. Among those pictured are Josephine Rodrigues, Nancy Y'Barbo, and Sylvia Montes. (Courtesy of Sacred Heart Catholic Church.)

Prepared to make a short trip to the neighboring farm of her brother-in-law Manuel Molandes, Lois Lazarine Molandes and her son Grady Molandes are shown with their main mode of transportation, their horse. Robert Molandes, her husband, left for the U.S. Army in 1942 when Grady was three weeks old. She lived in the Eden community with Robert's brother Hood Molandes and his wife, Gladys Mora Molandes. (Courtesy of Jan Dobbs Barton.)

Many young ladies in the county supported the war effort by working at Mize Factory, attending events at the local USO, and writing to the soldiers they met. Pictured are, from left to right, Virginia Molandes Heady, Jean Molandes Trautwein, Lorena Molandes Dobbs, and Ruby Molandes Dobbs. Trautwein was still in grammar school during the war but the others worked in the factories. (Courtesy of Velma Molandes Miller.)

Many young men and women supported the war effort by moving to the Gulf Coast to work in the shipyards and other factories. Pictured in Houston are a group of workers early in the war. On the far right are Jack Zscheck and Leola Molanders, who later married. During the war, Jack served in the U.S. Navy as a Japanese message decoder. (Courtesy of Jan Dobbs Barton.)

Prepare For

BLACKOUT

FRIDAY NIGHT!

Nacogdoches will have a trial "blackout" Friday night, December 19, in keeping with the desires of the Office of Civilian Defense and of Governor Stevenson.

THE TIME WILL BE BETWEEN 8 and 10 P. M.

It is being done under the direction of the city and county officials.

Follow the details of the requirements in the Daily Sentinel and the Redland Herald.

ABOVE ALL . . . DO NOT GET EXCITED AND LOSE YOUR HEAD . . . THAT WOULD BE THE WORST POSSIBLE THING TO DO AT ANY TIME!

On Friday, December 19, 1941, Nacogdoches experienced its first blackout in keeping with the Office of Civilian Defense and Texas governor Coke Robert Stevenson. The blackout lasted two hours between 8 p.m. and 10 p.m. Polly Jeffries Ritterskamp and her cousin were driving downtown when the lights went out. She remembers parking on the side of the street until the lights were turned on. In 1942, Polly moved to Fort Worth to go to work with Consolidated Aircraft in Fort Worth, Texas, where she riveted airplanes. In this photograph, Polly—a real Rosie the Riveter—is rushing to catch a bus with her bandana in hand. (Above, courtesy of ETRC, SFASU; left, courtesy of Polly Jeffries Ritterskamp.)

Nine

Our Veterans Fight for Liberty

Local historian and author, Francis Edward "Ab" Abernethy (standing, far left), 17, joined the U.S. Navy in the spring of 1943, just after graduation from NHS. He was assigned to the USS *Harkness*, a wooden-hulled, minesweeper serving as a survey ship. In this photograph, Abernethy and his crew are fully armed on the west coast of Okinawa in 1945. (Courtesy of Edward Abernethy.)

After Pearl Harbor was bombed in 1941, recruitment for young men in the U.S. Army began immediately. By the end of that year, President Roosevelt had signed an amendment to the Selective Service Act to require all men between the ages of 18 and 64 to register for the draft, and men between the ages of 20 and 44 were subject to service. This new measure forced seven million men to register and begin preparing for war duties. This advertisement appeared frequently in the *Daily Sentinel* as a reminder to all. (Courtesy of the National Archives.)

Fritz Guy Adams, brother to Berdine Adams, and his niece Retha Christine Adams are shown here with their spouses. Adams and his wife, Opal Merrell, are on the left; Retha and her husband, August Lester Tubbe, are on the right. Adams served in the U.S. Navy and Tubbe served in the U.S. Army during the war. (Courtesy of Frank Adams.)

Pfc. Leo Acosta (third from left), 22, and John Arroya (far right), 17, created a special bond while serving together as artillery gunners in Europe. Not hearing from each other for 60 years, in 2005, Arroya began searching for his old friend and found him in Nacogdoches. Their reunion was bittersweet, as most of the men they served with had died. Their friendship forged in war has been a forever friendship. (Courtesy of Leo Acosta.)

Pvt. George Arriola, 21, of the U.S. Army, was serving with the 2nd Division, 23rd Infantry Regiment when it invaded Normandy Beach on June 7, 1944, D-Day plus 1. He fought with his unit through the hedgerows of France, until September 24, 1944, when he was wounded at Brest, France. He spent eight months in hospitals in England and Texas before he was released in May 1945. (Courtesy of Brinda Arriola McClain.)

James Arriola (far right) smiles with his buddies from the USS *Pickens* while relaxing in Honolulu, Hawaii, in January 1945. One month later, Arriola was ferrying U.S. Marines in a wooden Higgins boat to the shores of Iwo Jima amidst constant bombings. He remembers seeing the Japanese *Zeros* and thinking "Hell, this is war!" His brothers Richard, Joe A., and Leo also served in World War II. (Courtesy of James Arriola.)

Richard "Buddy" Anderson (right), 22, and his younger brother Ernest "Buck" Anderson (left) both died in World War II. They were Cushing High School students from Lilbert. Buddy died on June 10, 1944, in Italy and is buried at the Sicily-Rome American Cemetery. His little brother Buck died on May 21, 1945, in Okinawa and is buried at the National Memorial Cemetery of the Pacific in Honolulu, Hawaii. (Courtesy of SFASU Alumni Association.)

Cullis Rayford Wilson (left) and Bennett Perkins Blake took this photograph while awaiting discharge from the U.S. Marine Corps on January 9, 1946. They were both survivors of the Battle of Iwo Jima and graduated from NHS. Wilson currently lives in Chireno; Blake died on March 2, 1998. (Courtesy of the Blake Family and ETRC, SFASU.)

Six of the 24 young men who played in the 1939 NHS winning football team died in World War II. One of these men was Torpedo Mate Charles Lee Brantley, 19, who graduated from high school in 1940. He entered the U.S. Navy in October 1940 and served on the USS *Atlanta*. He had been in the Pacific nine months before he was reported missing in action and presumed dead on November 13, 1942. (Courtesy of Joyce Bright Swearingen.)

Another of the young 1939 NHS football players was Cadet Major "M. F." Russell. After graduating from NHS in 1940, he attended Texas A&M University and SFASTC before joining the U.S. Army Air Corps in 1942. He was stationed at Ellington Air Base in San Antonio as an aviation cadet when he died in a plane crash on February 15, 1943. A letter written to his mother by teammate Thurman Talley said, "His life was voluntarily placed on the altar of service to his country and to God; than this there is no greater glory." Ironically, later that year Talley was also killed in a similar plane crash. (Courtesy of Joyce Bright Swearingen.)

Identified in this family photograph are, from left to right, (first row), M.Sgt. Novell George "N. G." Bright, Joyce Bright, and Charles Bright, all children of Novell and Dovie Bright (second row). The photograph was taken when N. G. was home from the Pacific War in November 1942. After his furlough, he went to officer training school and then to the war in North Africa. (Courtesy of Joyce Bright Swearingen.)

Like father, like son: On May 14, 1945, Pvt. John Robert Cason landed at the U.S. Marine Corps training base in Parris Island, South Carolina, to enter boot camp. His father, Robert Nance Cason, had arrived on May 17, 1917, to begin his boot camp training during World War I nearly 28 years earlier. (Courtesy of Barbara Cason Merlie.)

Three brothers—Oscar, Frankie (pictured left), and Tommy Chireno (pictured right with his daughter Grace)—sons of Joe and Francis Gonzales Chireno, all served in the U.S. Army during World War II. Tommy enlisted in 1942 and served in Africa; Oscar enlisted in 1944 and served in Italy; and Frankie enlisted in 1945 as the war neared its end. Frankie and Tommy were married to sisters Nellie and Hazel Molandes. (Courtesy of Jan Dobbs Barton and Velma Molandes Miller.)

African American men of the community asked for the opportunity to fight in the war. They believed it to be their right to participate in the defense of their country in the same manner and on the same basis as other Americans. Leo Colson was one of those men. He served proudly as a truck driver in an engineering regiment in the European Theater of Operations. (Courtesy of Karen Colston Ballard.)

T.Sgt. Calvin Wesley "C. W." Copeland of Nacogdoches landed on Normandy Beach on July 7, 1944, D-Day plus 2. He served in Iceland, England, France, and Belgium before his discharge in 1945. Copeland (right) is shown in front of a captured Nazi flag with a buddy. (Courtesy of Linda Greer.)

Sgt. Burleson Corley, 24, from Sacul died June 2, 1945, in the Philippines. His body was brought back after the war and he was buried in the Sacul Cemetery. Corley's family suffered another loss when his brother Ralph was killed in the Korean War on October 18, 1952. (Courtesy of the SFA Alumni Association.)

John Cortines, of the U.S. Army, was drafted at the age of 21. He was assigned as a truck driver to the 298th Engineer Combat Battalion, Company C in Northern Europe. His unit had the task of removing numerous roadblocks, obstacles, and minefields that were hindering the advance of the leading combat units. (Courtesy of John Douglas Cortines.)

Benjamin Cortines, 18, joined the Coast Guard in 1943 and served in the Asiatic-Pacific theater at Leyte, Luzon, and Iwo Jima aboard the USS *Calloway*. This undated recruitment photograph reads, "Seaman Cortines is very enthusiastic about the part the Coast Guard played in the Marshall (Islands) invasion and is looking ahead to others where he hopes he will have an active part." (Courtesy of Bernard Garcia.)

A U.S. soldier stands in front of bodies at the Dachau, Germany, concentration camp on April 29, 1945. The camp was the first set up by the Nazis in 1933 and was used as a prototype for others. The camp held 32,000 prisoners on the day of liberation by Americans. (Photograph by Capt. W. D. Murdy; courtesy of ETRC, SFASU.)

Pfc. Claude Daniel, from Woden, was also at the Dachau Concentration Camp in April 1945 when this photograph was taken. His simple words on the back of the photograph tell the whole story, "It is hard to believe, but it is so." (Courtesy of Stacy Jacobs Borders.)

Baker Denman, 17, passed an officer's candidate test while a senior at NHS and joined the U.S. Navy in April 1943, attending officer training school at Southwestern Louisiana Institute. Upon graduation, he was assigned to a patrol craft in the Pacific. His longtime friend, Ab Abernethy, remembers meeting Denman at Pearl Harbor once where they had a chew of Days Work tobacco and a good visit. (Courtesy of Edward Francis Abernethy.)

Cleon "Buck" Fausett, 18, an NHS football player and graduate, was drafted into the U.S. Navy in 1943. He spent four years in the South Pacific aboard the USS LST-747. Upon returning home, he went to work as a salesman for Big Dutchman and later DeWitt Hatcheries. In recent years, Fausett has been active in the board of directors of the scholarship program of the NHS Alumni Association. (Courtesy of Buck Fausett.)

Capt. John Jack Forman was in the Allied invasion of Normandy Beach on June 6, 1944. He chronicled his war stories in photographs and is seen here developing film in the battlefields of France. He commanded a POW camp in Ludwigsborg, Germany, and earned a Silver Star for his service in the Allied invasion of Omaha Beach. (Photograph by Capt. John Jack Forman; courtesy of the ETRC, SFASU.)

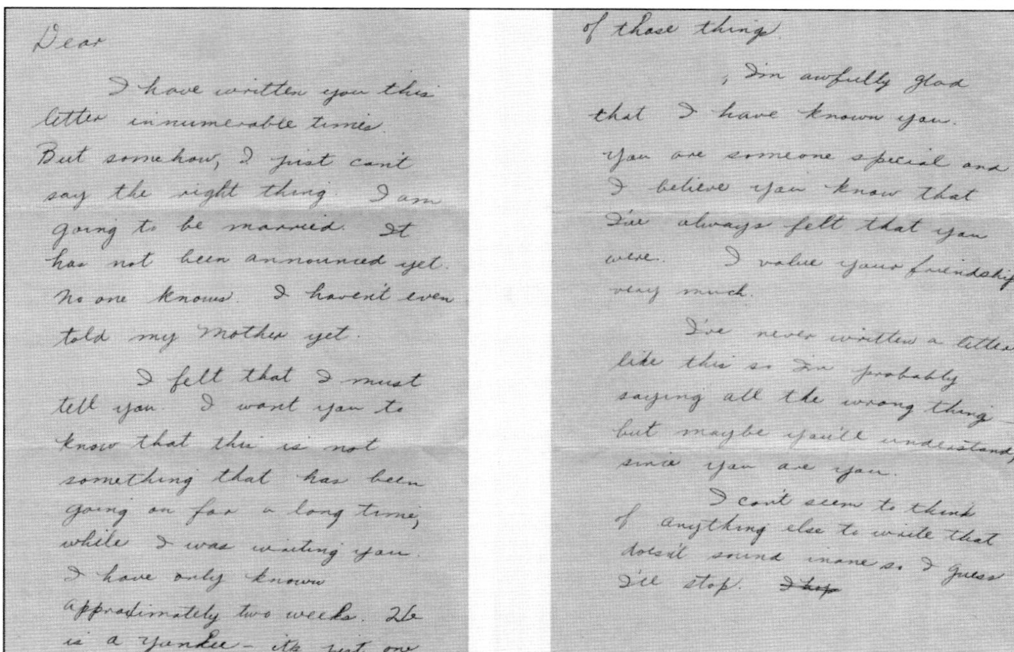

Dear

I have written you this letter innumerable times. But somehow, I just can't say the right thing. I am going to be married. It has not been announced yet. No one knows. I haven't even told my mother yet.

I felt that I must tell you. I want you to know that this is not something that has been going on for a long time, while I was writing you. I have only known approximately two weeks. He is a Yankee – it's just one of those things.

, I'm awfully glad that I have known you. You are someone special and I believe you know that I've always felt that you were. I value your friendship very much.

I've never written a letter like this so I'm probably saying all the wrong things – but maybe you'll understand, since you are you.

I can't seem to think of anything else to write that doesn't sound inane so I guess I'll stop. ~~I hope~~

During the war, "Dear John" letters were written frequently by young ladies to inform a boyfriend that their relationship was over. Most of the time, it was because the author had fallen for someone else and was to marry soon. When a soldier opened a letter and read the words "I don't know how to write this" or "I've started this letter a hundred times," they knew what was to come was not good news. (Courtesy of Nancy Tipton.)

Just out of high school at the age of 17, McNeil Grimes Jr. went to work for the Northern Indiana Brass Foundry Company, Inc., (NIBCO) in 1943. He was drafted into the U.S. Navy in 1945 and served in the Philippines. He was released early because his job at NIBCO was classified as necessary for defense of the nation. After 50 years of dedicated service, Grimes retired from NIBCO in 1993. (Courtesy of McNeil Grimes.)

Emmery "Ed" Hancock, 18, entered the U.S. Navy in 1945 and was in basic training at San Diego U.S. Naval Training Station when the last battle in the South Pacific was fought. After training, he became involved in the final phase of World War II. (Courtesy of Marie Hancock.)

Pfc. Joseph Barham "Jodie" Hargis, 18, a 1943 football player and graduate of NHS, was in the 3rd Armored Amphibious Battalion of the U.S. Marines Corps when he died at the Battle of Peleliu on October 16, 1944, at the age of 19. The National Museum of the Marine Corps calls this battle "the bitterest battle of the war for the Marines." (Courtesy of Troy Hargis.)

Travis Shirley Helpenstell, of Mahl, was called the "Audie Murphy of Nacogdoches" by his friends. At 18, he joined the U.S. Marine Corps in 1943 and served in the South Pacific. In one incident, his heroism saved the lives of many of his fellow soldiers and caused the death of 27 Japanese combatants. After returning home to Nacogdoches, he became the youngest constable ever elected in Texas at the time. (Courtesy of Edward Abernethy.)

Charles Lee Hill, a SFASTC graduate, wrote for camp newspapers, led a medical detachment dance band, and composed music for camp shows while in the U.S. Army. The highlight of his career was the composition of "Space City, U.S.A.," a tribute to the Space Center in Houston. The piece premiered at the reception for Pres. John F. Kennedy at the Houston airport in 1962. (Courtesy of ETRC, SFASU.)

Pfc. Raymond Hutchison, far right, joined the U.S. Army in 1942 and served in France and Germany. His younger brother Leon, far left, entered the U.S. Army at the end of the war. Also pictured are their youngest brother, Glen, and their parents, Walter and Effie Hutchison. This photograph was taken when Raymond came home on leave to marry Margaret Dobbs in August 1943. (Courtesy of June Hutchison Huffman.)

Billie Wayne Jacobs, 19, was in the U.S. Army in 1944 when he was injured by a grenade explosion in Southern France and lost his left leg. In 1947, the federal government gave him a new Oldsmobile 88 with an automatic transmission, which enabled him to drive. In this photograph, he is shown with the new car in front of N. W. Smith's car dealership. (Courtesy of Dorothy King Jacobs.)

Joseph W. Kennedy, a NHS and SFASTC graduate, received his Ph.D. from the University of California in 1939. The following year, he, along with Glenn Seaborg, Edwin McMillan, and Arthur Wahl, discovered plutonium. In March 1943, he entered Project Y at Los Alamos National Laboratory where he was on the Manhattan Project team that produced the first atomic bomb, which ultimately ended the war. (Courtesy of SFA Alumni Association.)

Franklin Leonard Sr. was 27 when he joined the U.S. Army in 1939 and had already spent four years in the U.S. Navy. Well trained when the war began, he was recruited to join a special team that used unique talents to mislead and deceive the Germans. Although he never spoke of his mission during the war, his family believes he may have been part of the "Ghost Army" whose mission was to draw fire away from the real U.S. Army troops. After the war was over, he was discharged for a few years before he enlisted in the U.S. Army Air Force, from which he retired in 1963. (Courtesy of Franklin Leonard Jr.)

Cpl. Joe Lopez Jr. was a U.S. Marine during World War II when he was wounded in action during the Battle at Iwo Jima. He also participated in battles at Okinawa, Ryukyu Island, and the occupation of China. He remained in the U.S. Marine Corps Reserves after being discharged. (Courtesy of Rita Lopez Muckleroy.)

Home from the U.S. Army in about 1943, Pfc. Louis Luna poses with the Luna family. Pictured, from left to right, are (first row) Thomas, James, Louis, and Marie; (second row) Velma, mother Laney, father Jack, Mary, Lonnie, and Robert. Louis joined the U.S. Army in May 1943 and served as a medical technician with the 603 Medical Clearing Company. He was discharged in December 1945. (Courtesy of Thomas Luna.)

Pharmacist's Mate First Class Alonzo "A. L." Mangham Jr. was awarded the Silver Star in 1944 for "conspicuous gallantry" and "disregard of his own safety" while serving as a member of a medical company landing team on the Island of Saipan in the Mariana Islands. A career military man, he joined the U.S. Marines in February 1941 and served in World War II, the Korean War, and helped train Navy SEALs for the Vietnam War. He retired in 1960 from the U.S. Navy with the rank of lieutenant commander. (Courtesy of City of Nacogdoches.)

Eight months after he was drafted into the U.S. Army, on November 11, 1944, Pvt. Floyd Molandes was killed in action on the Ruhr River in Germany. He served under Maj. Gen. Terry Allen, Company I, 413th Infantry Regiment, 104th Infantry Division, 3rd Battalion, better known as the Timberwolves. He was buried at the Henri-Chapelle American Cemetery in Belgium until 1947 when his body was returned to the United States aboard the USS *Joseph V. Connolly*. On November 20, 1947, his remains were the first of many to arrive in Nacogdoches that year. From the train depot, his casket was pulled by a jeep down Main Street to Oakley Metcalf Funeral Home. The convoy was preceded by a color guard, three drummers, and the post chaplain of the VFW as a low rumble of "Taps" was played. (Courtesy of Jan Dobbs Barton.)

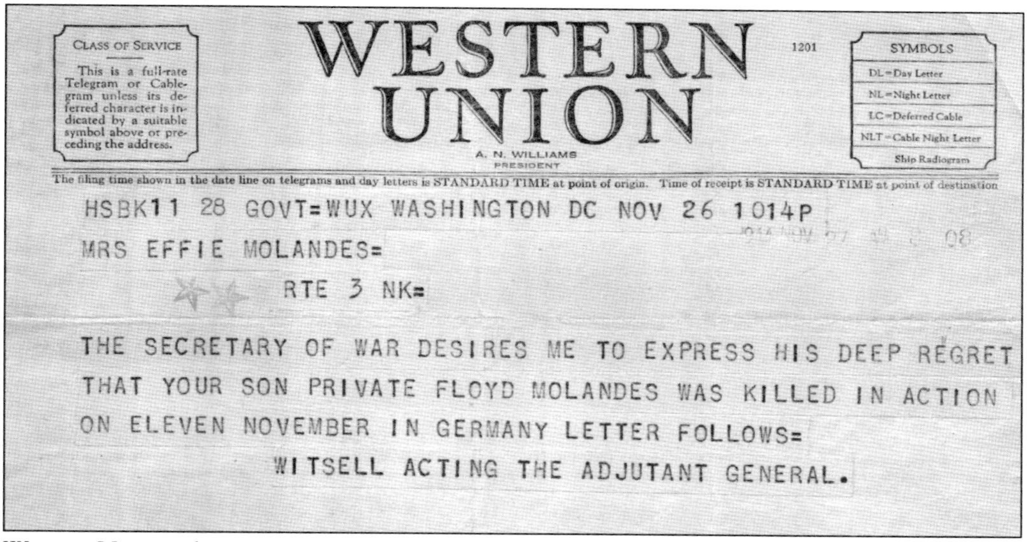

CLASS OF SERVICE
This is a full-rate Telegram or Cablegram unless its deferred character is indicated by a suitable symbol above or preceding the address.

WESTERN UNION

A. N. WILLIAMS
PRESIDENT

1201

SYMBOLS
DL=Day Letter
NL=Night Letter
LC=Deferred Cable
NLT=Cable Night Letter
Ship Radiogram

The filing time shown in the date line on telegrams and day letters is STANDARD TIME at point of origin. Time of receipt is STANDARD TIME at point of destination

HSBK11 28 GOVT=WUX WASHINGTON DC NOV 26 1014P

MRS EFFIE MOLANDES=

RTE 3 NK=

THE SECRETARY OF WAR DESIRES ME TO EXPRESS HIS DEEP REGRET THAT YOUR SON PRIVATE FLOYD MOLANDES WAS KILLED IN ACTION ON ELEVEN NOVEMBER IN GERMANY LETTER FOLLOWS=

WITSELL ACTING THE ADJUTANT GENERAL.

Western Union telegrams announcing the deaths of servicemen were sent to the local newspaper office and then delivered by newspaper employees. During World War II, families always dreaded a knock on the door, as it almost always meant bad news. This telegram, sent to Effie Molandes, Floyd Molandes' mother, is dated November 26, 1944. It reported the death of her son on November 11, 1944, in Germany. (Courtesy of Jan Dobbs Barton.)

Most soldiers killed in World War II did not return home but were buried in memorial cemeteries throughout the world. For those families who wanted their sons returned home, the federal government started bringing in their remains in 1947. This rare photograph, taken at the funeral of Floyd Molandes, captures a moment of sorrow played out in far too many communities across the nation. (Courtesy of Jan Dobbs Barton.)

Jessie Molandes, uncle of Floyd Molandes, entered the U.S. Army in March 1941 and trained in the Chemical Warfare School. He is pictured here with his brothers. From left to right are (first row) Jessie, Robert, and Edd; (second row) Manuel, Hood, Jack, and Dave. Jessie's brother Robert, his brother-in-law Frankie Chireno, and two other nephews—Joe Molandes and Philip Arriola—also served in the Great War. (Courtesy of Fannie Molandes Wardlaw.)

Joseph Leo Molandes, son of Manuel and Effie Cloudy Molandes, is pictured here with his sister Lorena. He joined the U.S. Army Air Corps in 1942, serving in a medical unit in Lincoln, Nebraska. His service was often overshadowed by the death of his brother Floyd in Europe in 1944, but their family was proud of both boys. Joe married Rose Manchack in 1947 and died of cancer in 1950 at the age of 28. (Courtesy of Jan Dobbs Barton.)

Assigned to the 54th evacuation hospital unit as a litter bearer, Robert Molandes (left) sits in front of a field aid station in the Philippines. First echelon medical service in combat situations included emergency medical treatment in the field, removal of battle casualties, and establishment of aid stations for the reception, triage, temporary care, and treatment of casualties. (Courtesy of Lois Lazarine Molandes.)

Pfc. Sylvester Molandes joined the U.S. Army in November 1941 and served in the 559th Signal Air Warning Battalion in Europe as a radio operator. After the war, he moved to Aberdeen, Washington, and married Cora Underwood in 1953. He lived his life there but was brought "home" to Nacogdoches for burial in Bonaldo Cemetery in 1983. (Courtesy of Lois Lazarine Molandes.)

Pfc. Gaston Montes was drafted into the U.S. Army in November 1942 at the age of 20. After his basic training in Oregon, California, Arizona, and Colorado, he was assigned to the U.S. Army's Headquarters Company, 413th Infantry Regiment, 104th Infantry Division, better known as the Timberwolves. On October 29, 1944, near Zundert, Holland, Montes was wounded, and Lt. Col. Peter Denisevich was the first to reach him and get him to safety. The two men forged a friendship that day that lasted all their lives. Montes kept up with his Timberwolf buddies, until his death in 1997, by attending their annual reunions regardless of where they were held. (Courtesy of Gloria Montes.)

Lt. Jack Moore Jr. entered the U.S. Navy in June 1942 and trained at the U.S. Navy Amphibious Base in the Philippines. He served at Attu, Kiska, Saipan, Tinian, and Leyte. (Courtesy of Esterlene Blacksher Moore.)

T.Sgt. Wilson Muckleroy entered the U.S. Army Air Corps in October 1941 and trained to be an airplane and engine mechanic. He served stateside during the war as a B-29 crew chief for 10 airplanes, as shown in this photograph. After discharge, he ran his own businesses until 1958 when he started a 25-year career with the U.S. Postal Service as a rural mail carrier. (Courtesy of Johnny Shivers.)

Local comedian and bigger-than-life character Bob Murphey lost his arm as a young boy; however, he never let his handicap interfere with his life. When the war broke out, he went to sign up to fight just like all of his friends but was told he could not join. Not taking "no" as a final answer, he continued to ask until finally he was allowed to join the U.S. Merchant Marines and later the U.S. Maritime Service's Hospital Corps. (Courtesy of Reba Jane Gayler.)

Bernard Joseph Packard was drafted into the U.S. Army in September 1944 and served as a Tech 4 in the 35th Transportation Corps Service Group. His ship, the USS *General John Pope*, operated in the South Pacific and provided antiaircraft, or AA, gun support to American troops during the assault on Luzon. Packard later became the president and chief executive officer of Bluewater Industries in Houston. (Courtesy of the Packard family.)

Boat Mate 1st Class Eugene Mora joined the U.S. Navy in February 1941 and spent the next 20 years in service for his country. During World War II, he was assigned to the USS *Altair* out of Mare Island, California, and was a Master-at-Arms, a ranking in the U.S. Navy's military police. He experienced one ship sunk out from under him and a close call on another. (Courtesy of Zee Mora Stone.)

Cpl. James Orland Pitts, 19, was with the 3rd U.S. Marine Corps Division at Bougainville on the Solomon Islands when he and one other soldier failed to return from a reconnaissance mission. He was listed as presumed dead on November 7, 1944. He is memorialized in the Manila American Cemetery and the Memorial in the Philippines. His cousin was Thomas Marvin Pitts, who was killed in action on January 24, 1942. (Courtesy of Mildred Lee Pitts.)

George Vernon Pruitt graduated from NHS in 1939 and entered the U.S. Army Air Corps in March 1941. He trained as a pilot at various locations throughout the nation and served in the China, Burma, and India Theater where he flew C47s over the Hump. For his "heroism or extraordinary achievement while participating in an aerial flight," he received the Distinguished Flying Cross. He retired in 1968 at the rank of lieutenant colonel. (Courtesy of Gary Woods and Lou Ann Pruitt Hoppe.)

The first soldier who died during World War II from Nacogdoches County was Pfc. Thomas Marvin Pitts, 27, the son of Jasper and Nettie Christopher Pitts. He was killed in action in the Battle of Bataan on January 24, 1942. Tragedy struck his family again when his first cousin, James Orland Pitts, was killed in action on November 7, 1944, on the Soloman Islands. (Courtesy of Jon Pitts.)

Bernice "Bernie" Pleasant was drafted into the U.S. Army Air Corps in 1941, became a pilot, and retired 33 years later as a colonel. He served in World War II, Korea, and Vietnam. On June 6, 1944, D-Day, he was part of the airborne assault that dropped paratroopers behind enemy lines. (Courtesy of Delores Kot Pleasant.)

S.Sgt. Hubert Poskey, 19, entered the U.S. Army in September 1943 and served in the 6th Army, 37th Division, 140th Field Artillery Battery. He received his basic training at Camp Roberts in California and his first assignment was in the South Pacific, where he arrived at Bougainville Island on Easter Sunday, 1944. (Courtesy of Peggy Arriola Jasso.)

On one of the battlefields in Okinawa, Sgt. James Poskey and a buddy were in a fox hole when they were attacked by a Japanese officer wielding a samurai sword. Unfortunately James' buddy was killed by blows from the sword but James shot the man and lived to tell the story. James' primary duty in the Philippines was to clear caves with a flamethrower. (Courtesy of James Poskey.)

Cpl. Vert Poskey, 18, was drafted into the U.S. Army Air Corps in June 1943 and received his basic training at Kearns, Utah, and Camp Lee, Virginia, before being assigned to the 13th Army Air Corps, 6th Photo Technician Squadron. His squadron developed the aerial photographs taken by reconnaissance planes. (Courtesy of Vert Poskey.)

While writing letters home in New Delhi, India, Pfc. John Louis Schmidt (right), of the U.S. Army Signal Corps, ran into a friend from Nacogdoches, Dan Davison. They enjoyed 10 days of catching up on news and took a photograph published in the *Daily Sentinel* in July 1945. Maj. Henry Phillip Schmidt Jr. (left), John's brother, served in the U.S. Army Air Corps and was stationed in Puerto Rico. (Courtesy of Dena Schmidt Johnson.)

In June 1939, Norris Edward Smith, 16, joined the U.S. Army serving as platoon sergeant at Camp Wolters, then as a certified parachute rigger/instructor at Ft. Benning. Smith, shown here demonstrating the M1 rifle, trained 780 infantry soldiers in 13 platoons, trained 625 jumpers, and certified 3,125 parachutes. In August 1945, he was headed to California to eventually parachute into Japan as part of the invasion forces. He credits the atomic bomb with saving his life. (Courtesy of Edward Smith.)

Tommy and James, brothers to Edward Smith, also served in the U.S. Army during World War II. Once when Tommy was asked why young men from Nacogdoches volunteered for the service, his answer was, "life in the Army during World War II was easier than the life on the farm during the Great Depression years." (Courtesy of Edward Smith.)

Pfc. Archie Rison Sr., 20, entered the U.S. Army in June 1943 and served in the 3215th Quartermaster Service unit as a heavy truck driver. He served in Northern France, Ardennes, Rhineland, and Central Europe during the war. An executive order to integrate the military was not signed until July 26, 1948, by Pres. Harry S. Truman. (Courtesy of Archie Rison Jr.)

Pfc. John "Little Rod" Rodrigues was a 1943 graduate of NHS and a member of the famous 1939 football team. He was drafted into the U.S. Army and assigned to a hospital in Australia where he ministered to the sick and dying. Ironically John became ill and died on March 1, 1945, from an unknown disease he contracted in the hospital. (Courtesy of Tommie Rodrigues Montes.)

Sgt. John Lamar Satterwhite, 24, from Cushing, died on December 30, 1944, as he parachuted into Italy. Unconfirmed reports state that his brother was in the unit that recovered his body. He is buried at the Fenton Cemetery. (Courtesy of SFASU Alumni Association.)

Pvt. Lenard Self, 22, had the worst day of his life on Christmas Eve 1944 when his unit retreated during the Battle of the Bulge in Germany. He remembered almost freezing to death in snow about 30 inches deep. Self was assigned to I Company, 313 Infantry Battalion of the 79th Infantry Division. (Courtesy of Mary Lea White.)

On August 10, 1945, Amos Ben Simmons (left) and three buddies were on the Island of IE Shima, north of Okinawa, Japan, when this photograph was taken. The airplane in the background was a Japanese Betty bomber that had brought Japanese officials to board a C-54 transport. They then flew to the Philippines to meet with General McArthur and negotiate the peace plan to end the war. (Courtesy of Jerry Simmons.)

The Silver Star, the second highest medal awarded during World War II, was given for gallantry and heroism in action. In this photograph, taken in France, the Silver Star is being pinned on S.Sgt. Richard Solise, of the 1st Battalion, 23rd Infantry Regiment, by Maj. Gen. Walter Robertson, commander general of the 2nd Division. He received the award for "repelling the enemy attack on his battalion" on June 12, 1944. (Courtesy of Aaron Paul Solise.)

S.Sgt. William "Bill" Stegall, 20, from Big Rock near Cushing, was a tail gunner on a B-17 Flying Fortress in the 600th Squadron. He was 19 years old when he was killed instantly when a shrapnel fragment struck him in the back of the head. The tragedy occurred March 18, 1945, while the heavy bombardment group was on a raid over Berlin. (Courtesy of SFA Alumni Association.)

Sgt. Curtis Tarry, 31, from Nat, was a member of the 169th Infantry Regiment of the U.S. Army. He was killed on January 28, 1945, as the 43rd Division made an assault landing on the Luzon islands. His brother Sgt. Sam Tarry served in the U.S. Army Air Corps on Fiji and Iwo Jima and later became a partner at Axley and Rode, a CPA firm in Lufkin, Texas. (Courtesy SFA Alumni Association.)

Oscar Tigner, 25, entered the U.S. Army in February 1941. He served in the 393rd Quartermaster Truck Company in the Philippines, New Guinea, and North Solomon Islands as a heavy truck driver. Over 125,000 African American men served their country with distinction during World War II, and Oscar was one of those men. (Courtesy of Judge Dorothy Tigner Thompson.)

Brothers James Tipton (right) and John Tipton both served: James in the U.S. Marine Corps on the USS *St. Louis* and John in the U.S. Army. John's final moments were detailed in a letter written to his mother, Maude Tipton, by a fellow soldier who was with him at the time of his death in Europe in 1944. James returned to Nacogdoches after the war and became the owner of Tipton Ford. (Courtesy of Nancy Tipton.)

Ens. Anne Yerkovich, of the U.S. Navy, and Dr. Curtis Wallace, Navy Officer in the Medical/Dental Corps, were married in the Naval Academy chapel in Annapolis, Maryland, in December 1945. She was Head of Clothing and Small Stores at Norfolk Navy Air Station. He served in the invasions of Tarawa, Saipan, and Tinian in the South Pacific. They later made their home in Nacogdoches, where Wallace practiced dentistry. (Courtesy of Millicent Wallace Pitts.)

Travis Whitaker, of Cushing, is shown here with his wife, Auline. He entered the U.S. Navy in 1944 and served 18 months on a South Pacific island at command headquarters where he received and sent coded messages for all the South Pacific area. After the war, he completed his bachelor's and master's degrees at SFASTC where he later became an accountant and then auditor. He retired from SFASU as business manager in 1980. (Courtesy of Charles and Peggy Whitaker.)

Sgt. W. T. Williamson was in the 497th Bomber Squadron, 344th Bomber Group of the U.S. Army Air Corps when he was killed on February 23, 1945, in Holland. He is buried at the Netherlands American Cemetery in Margraten, Holland. (Courtesy of the SFA Alumni Association.)

Ten

Let the Good Times Roll

EXTRA **The Daily Sentinel** EXTRA

JAPANESE SURRENDER TO ALLIES

Japs Are Prodded Into Final Action By B-29 Raids

Pearl Harbor's Lights Go On

Japanese Were Out-Thought, Out-Guessed And Out-Fought

Truman's Announcement Expected Soon After 8 a. m. World Begins Celebrating

Washington, Tuesday, Aug. 14—Tokyo broadcasts reported early today that Japan has accepted the Allied unconditional surrender demand, but no Allied confirmation is likely before 8 a. m., (CWT).

If the enemy reports are true, World War II is over except for the formal signing of surrender documents by the defeated Japanese.

(An Office of War Information dispatch based on a Federal Communications Commission recording said flatly that the Japanese government had accepted the surrender terms).

The announcement came at 2:49 p. m. Tuesday, Tokyo time—90 hours and 19 minutes after Tokyo radio first broadcast Japan's surrender offer.

It means that the Japs gave up just three years, eight months and one week to the day that their "infamy at Pearl Harbor" plunged the United States into a two-front war that cost countless lives and billions of dollars.

It means that Japan can retain Emperor Hirohito—but that he must take orders from the Allied supreme commander to be named to administer to Japan. Gen. Douglas MacArthur is expected

The surrender of Japan to the Allies as pronounced in this *Daily Sentinel Extra* dated August 14, 1945, was a great victory for the American "doughboys" and a relief to their families. The actual surrender ceremony was held on the deck of the USS *Missouri* on September 2 when Gen. Douglas MacArthur accepted the Japanese Instrument of Surrender from the Japanese government, ending World War II. (Courtesy of ETRC, SFASU.)

Upon their return in 1946, the male and female veterans of World War II felt it necessary to organize a Veterans Club at SFASTC. The purpose was to aid the returning veterans in coping with pressing problems facing them as ex-GIs. They used the motto, "One for all and all for one" to carry out the tremendous undertaking as a combined effort. (Courtesy of ETRC, SFASU.)

John William "J. W." Lazarine of Nacogdoches (right) and George Tarver sit on the famous Spanish Steps in Rome, Italy, holding a newspaper announcing Victory in Europe, also called VE Day. May 8, 1945, marked the date when the Western Allies formally accepted the unconditional surrender of the armed forces of Nazi Germany. (Courtesy of Ginger Lazarine Johnson.)

Sammy Luna (far right) and friends were a part of the U.S. troops assigned to the occupation of Japan. They are shown here posing with a geisha in Tokyo, Japan. Sammy met his wife, Patricia McCarren, while she was working at the U.S. Army Post Exchange at Fort Momouth, New Jersey. (Courtesy of Sammy Luna.)

Serving in the U.S. Navy as part of the occupation forces, Sam Peyton McClain (right) is photographed with a buddy at the Rocker-Four Club in Tokyo, Japan. Sam graduated from Stephen F. Austin Demonstration School in 1949 after playing football at NHS for three years. Soon after graduation, he joined the U.S. Navy. (Courtesy of Mike McClain.)

James "Buck" Lee, 17, served in the 6th Marine Corps Division, 82nd Airborne in the South Pacific and then in Okinawa where he was wounded two days before his 20th birthday. Upon his return home, he finished college on the GI Bill and became active in helping veterans with their benefits. He served as the Nacogdoches County Veterans Affairs Officer for more than 20 years. (Courtesy of Jimmy and Pam Lee.)

In 1944, SFASTC basketball coach Bob Shelton helped form the first VFW post in Nacogdoches and became its first post commander. Shelton was a World War I veteran, having served in the U.S. Army. This old house located on Hunter Street was purchased by the VFW and was its first permanent meeting place. In 1949, the building was renovated and it became the VFW's current home. (Courtesy of the VFW Post No. 3893.)

Faye Lindsey was the first president of the Ladies Auxiliary to the Veterans of Foreign Wars in 1946. The ladies live by their motto, "Honor the dead by helping the living." They have a history of serving the veterans of this country and the community as a testament to the sacrifices and commitment of every man and woman who has served in uniform. (Courtesy of the VFW Post No. 3893.)

In June 1948, the first major international crisis of the Cold War occurred when the Soviet Union blocked the Western Allies' railroads and roads. In response, the Allies organized the Berlin Airlift to carry supplies to the people in West Berlin. Lee Jerome Montes was sent to Germany to handle the shipment of supplies; while there, he met and married his German wife, Amanda Pfeuffer. (Courtesy of Gary Montes.)

In June 1949, U.S. Army veteran John Woods opened a service station on the corner of North Street and Starr Avenue. In later years, the Humble name was changed to Enco, then to Exxon. It was the first station in the United States to have an Exxon sign. In the front car are Jewell Sanford (driving), bottler for the local Coca-Cola plant, and Lloyd Morgan. (Courtesy of Gary Woods.)

Occupants of the Buzzard's Roost, a house on the north side of Starr Avenue at Mound Street, are at a Women's Recreation Center (WRC) dance in 1946. The veterans and their dates pictured are, from left to right, (first row) Curtis Metcalf, Margaret Lokey, Mary Slover, Jimmie Lee Prickett, Lavon Lovell, and Martha Price; (second row) C. C. Denman, John Lee Shofner, Edward Abernethy, Don Barkett, Baker Denman, and Cyril "Posty" Roberts. (Courtesy of Edward Abernethy.)

Veterans were anxious to start their lives anew, so sweethearts who had corresponded sometimes married quickly. William "Bill" Miller, who hailed from Palisade, Colorado, met Philip Arriola while they were serving in the U.S. Army in 1944, stationed in Louisiana. Arriola brought Miller home to Nacogdoches with him while on furlough, planning to introduce him to his sisters. Instead he met Velma Molandes, Philip's cousin, and they began writing letters when the men returned to their post. After Miller was discharged in December 1945, he came to Nacogdoches to court Velma in person, all under the watchful eye of her father, Manuel Molandes. They married in February 1946 (above) and left immediately for his family farm in Palisade. Arriola had married his sweetheart, Hester Slater, in September 1945 (right). (Above, courtesy of Jan Dobbs Barton; right, courtesy of Judy Arriola.)

After the war, businesses sprang up all over the county. One of those, in Garrison, was a Humble-Esso service station owned by veterans of World War II Albert Hudgins (left) and his brother Alfred (right). Also pictured are Bill Adkinson (center) and Lonnie Hudgins (kneeling), their cousin. All four men worked at the station that sold gas and oil and performed routine automobile repairs. (Courtesy of Randy Hudgins.)

T.Sgt. Clarence "Bo" McMichael, 23, a football player at Texas College in Tyler, joined the U.S. Army in 1943. Because of his education, he was assigned to the all "colored" 777th field artillery battalion. His unit fought in the European theater. Upon his return to Texas College, he won All-American status in football and later became a teacher and coach at E. J. Campbell High School and Nacogdoches High School. He is pictured standing on the left in the first row. (Courtesy of Clarence McMichael.)

Cpl. James Johnston, 17, joined the U.S. Marines Corps and served in the South Pacific for four years. After the war, he attended SFASTC on the GI Bill and graduated in 1951. He then went to work for the Central Heights School District where he spent 31 years as coach, teacher, principal, and finally superintendent. For this dedicated service, the school board voted in 2010 to name the James Johnston Gymnasium in his honor. (Courtesy of Mildred Lee Pitts.)

After the war, James Arriola took advantage of the educational opportunities offered by the GI Bill. He graduated from the Texas Barber College in Fort Worth in 1948 (below). Sixty-four years later, he is still cutting hair at his shop in Nacogdoches. The GI program trained nearly eight million returning veterans at a cost of $14.5 billion. (Courtesy of James Arriola.)

Electricians Mate 2nd Class Theodore "T. C." Dobbs Jr. joined the U.S. Navy in March 1943, served on the USS *Hutchins*, and fought at the battles of Iwo Jima and Okinawa. After a kamikaze boat attack, the *Hutchins* was left crippled and headed for repairs when the war in the Pacific ended. Pictured here at the family home in Central Heights in 1946 are, from left to right, T. C. Dobbs Sr., Sallie Mae Arnold Dobbs, Kathryn Dobbs Johnson, T. C. Dobbs Jr., Billy Dobbs, Margaret Dobbs Hutchison, and Bennie Dale Dobbs Fryman in front. T. C. Jr. helped to decommission the *Hutchins* in Seattle, then went to school in Tyler and returned to Nacogdoches and a job at the new radio station KOSF (below). He went to work for NIBCO in 1954, using his U.S. Navy electrician's training and experience until his retirement in 1990. (Both courtesy of Jan Dobbs Barton.)

Tom Barton, second from the left, was a well-known East Texas salesman who drove the back roads of Nacogdoches County selling road construction equipment. He was also a quadriplegic, injured in 1946 at the age of 17 in a diving accident. After years of hospitalization and therapy, he returned to graduate from Cushing High School in 1949 at the age of 21, where he was manager of the basketball team. (Courtesy of Jan Dobbs Barton.)

A new era began in April 1945 when Harry S. Truman became the 33rd president of the United States, replacing Franklin Delano Roosevelt who died in office. Truman will always be remembered as the president who made the decision to use nuclear weapons against Japan. In this photograph taken somewhere in East Texas, Truman appears to be on his whistle-stop campaign in 1948. (Courtesy of Stacy Jacobs Borders.)

The first and only Nacogdoches County man to die in Operation Iraqi Freedom as of 2010, Spc. Travis Wayne Buford, 23, son of Janet Buford of Douglass and Anthony Buford of New Braunfels, was laid to rest in the Douglass Cemetery on March 3, 2007. He died on February 22, 2007 from wounds he received the day before in the Al Anbar Province, a dangerous area of western Iraq. A gunner in the Multi-National Force-West, Buford's armored vehicle was hit by an improvised explosive device that killed him and two other men. He was with the 1st Battalion, 9th Infantry Regiment, 2nd Brigade Combat Team, 2nd Infantry Division. At his funeral, he was remembered by his family and U.S. Army officers as a fun-loving family man and a dutiful soldier. (Photograph by Kevin White; courtesy of the *Daily Sentinel*.)

NACOGDOCHES COUNTY CASUALTIES

Ernest D. Arrington
Ernest Buck Anderson
Richard Alvin Anderson
Bill Arriola
Amon Mack Blair
James Buck Blanton
William Henry Bobo
Charles Lee Brantley
James H. Brantley
Richard Dale Bray
March G. Bruton
Fred Gordan Buckner
Thomas Jefferson Clifton
Grover Cleveland Consford Jr.
Ivey Oquinn Cooper
Burleson Corley
Ollie T. Crump
Leon Wilson Davis
Albert Lee Dunks
Alfred Grady Edens Jr.
Travis Edwards
Alton Glen Estes
Eli Monroe Farrell
T. P. Flanagan
James Phillips Fleniken
Euell Alvin Forbis
Carl Travis Forney
Mirvle Everett Fulmer
George Glenn Gates
Jesse Gipson
Willie Daulton Griffin
Frank Holbert Hall
Joseph Barham Hargis
Robert Cook Herbert
Algy Iverson Herring
James Herbert Hinds
Odessa Holland
John W. Honeycutt
Elvyn Glynn Hopper
Marshall Hosea
Earl L. Huey
Guy Gable Jackson
Harold Lee Jeter
Lester Randolph Johnson
Obert E. Johnson
Dickey B. Johnston
Henry Franklin Jopling
Walter Mark Jordan Jr.
Joe A. Kasmiersky
Emmett King
James R. King
James C. Lane
John Aubrey Lea
R. Q. Pete Lester
Randolph Magruder Martin Jr.
Edsel Victor McIver
Mervil McCuistion
Robert Victor McCuistion
Bernard Franklin Milford
Frank Addo Miller
Jesse J. Miller
John Lee Miller
Floyd Molandes
Saint Elmo Bill Murdock
Charles Quentin Nix
Forrest Eugene Norton
James Carlton Owens
Mark Levon Parrish
Bernard Joseph Pena
Boyd Perry
Pink Elton Perry
Raymond Hal Phillips
James Orland Pitts
Thomas Marvin Pitts
Leslie Earl Poe
Walter Robin Ramsey
Clifton Randle
Roy James Rector
Hubert W Roberts
Floyd Patrick Rodrigues
John Athanasius Rodrigues
Roland Cleon Rogers
Major Frank Russell
James Edward Sachtleben
Harry Wilbern Sanford
Johnny Lamar Satterwhite
A. D. Scarbrough
Eugene L. Shoemaker
Dale D. Snelson
Ananisa Sparks
Chalmer Willis Spurgeon
William R. E. Stegall
Thurman Delma Talley
Curtis Robert Tarry
Clarence Thorn
Walter Arthur Thruston Jr.
John Maxey Tipton
Thomas Grant Touchstone
Luther Leon Vail
I. V. Watts
Loarn Wesley Weems
Walter C. Westbrook
Wilfred Gene Whitaker
Ben L. White
L. T. White
David Lloyd Whitley
Charles Richard Williams
W. T. Williamson
Ollie Yarborough